CENTRAL AMERICAN IMMIGRANTS
IN THEIR SHOES

BY PATRICIA HUTCHISON

Published by The Child's World®
1980 Lookout Drive • Mankato, MN 56003-1705
800-599-READ • www.childsworld.com

Content Consultant: Cecilia Menjívar, Professor, Department of Sociology,
University of California, Los Angeles

Photographs ©: Dario Lopez-Mills/AP Images, cover, 1; Pat Hamilton/AP Images, 6, 8;
Nick Ut/AP Images, 9; Kobby Dagan/Shutterstock Images, 10; Shutterstock Images,
12; Javier Garcia/Shutterstock Images, 14; Eduardo Verdugo/AP Images, 15; Eric Gay/
AP Images, 16, 20; Fernando Antonio/AP Images, 18; Red Line Editorial, 22; David
J. Phillip/AP Images, 24; Hans-Maximo Musielik/AP Images, 26; Alex Brandon/AP
Images, 27; Marie D. De Jes's/Houston Chronicle/AP Images, 28

ISBN 9781503827950
LCCN 2018944110

Printed in the United States of America
PA02394

ABOUT THE AUTHOR

Patricia Hutchison has written more than a dozen children's books about
history and science. She was a teacher for many years. Now she enjoys
volunteering as a reading tutor. She also spends time crafting and traveling
with her husband.

TABLE OF CONTENTS

FAST FACTS

Central American Countries

- Countries in Central America are Belize, Costa Rica, El Salvador, Guatemala, Honduras, Nicaragua, and Panama.

Why Central American Immigrants Left

- In Central America, there is a small group of very wealthy people who don't share the wealth with everyone else. This inequality has caused many people to leave.

- Civil wars in countries such as Guatemala and El Salvador have led to **persecution** of certain groups of people. Some nations in Central America are among the most violent in the world.

- Earthquakes and hurricanes have destroyed some cities and farmlands in Central America, leaving people to live in very poor conditions.

- Immigrants need documents from the U.S. government to live in the United States. However, some immigrants aren't able to get these documents. This is why some immigrants hire **coyotes** to help them get into the United States.

TIMELINE

1960: A civil war between the government and **guerrilla** groups begins in Guatemala. It lasts for 36 years.

1970s: **Refugees** begin to flow into the United States from Guatemala.

1980: El Salvador's civil war begins.

1990: Congress allows people from countries experiencing armed conflict or natural disasters to stay temporarily in the United States.

1998: Hurricane Mitch devastates Honduras and Nicaragua.

2009: The president of Honduras is arrested by the country's military. The new government begins arresting and hurting anyone who speaks against the government.

2015: Approximately 110,000 people from Honduras, Guatemala, and El Salvador seek **asylum** in the United States.

2018: The U.S. government commits to a zero-tolerance policy on illegal immigration. Under President Donald Trump, the government begins separating parents and children who illegally cross the U.S. border.

Chapter 1

FLEEING FROM CIVIL WAR

From the time she was 15 years old, Mercedes Garcia lived in fear. In 1980, a civil war began in El Salvador, her home country. The fighting was all around her. Bullets flew through the thin wood walls of her house. She would hide under the bed to get away from the conflict. Hiding made Mercedes feel safe, but she wasn't.

One day, soldiers came to Mercedes' house. They grabbed her brother and told him he was going to fight in the army. Their mother begged the men, with tears pouring down her face, to let her son go. She gave them all the money she had. Finally, they released the boy. Mercedes' parents were afraid the soldiers would come back. Her father decided to take his son to the United States so he wouldn't be forced to fight in the war.

Mercedes watched as her father and brother left. She was sad to see them go but happy they would finally be safe. Years went by. Mercedes married and had a son, but the war raged on. Power stations were bombed, and her family had no electricity for months. Mercedes decided to join her father and brother in the United States. She wanted to find a safe place to live. Then she would send for her husband and son.

In 1990, Mercedes said goodbye to her family. She went north with some neighbors. They had to sneak out of the country. They rode in buses and hid in the backs of trucks and trailers. When she crossed into Guatemala, her smuggler took them to a house. In the middle of the night, men with machine guns robbed them all. For the rest of the journey, Mercedes ate only the skimpy **rations** the coyotes gave her.

▲ **El Salvador's government troops were responsible for many civilian deaths during the civil war.**

After a month of travel, the group made it to the U.S. border. Because Mercedes didn't have the U.S. government's permission to enter the United States, she crossed the U.S. border by hiding in a car trunk. Another car picked her up and drove her to Colorado. When she first laid eyes on her father and brother, she ran to greet them. The peace and quiet in Colorado seemed strange to her. After living in a place where bombs and bullets were part of daily life, she enjoyed the soft sounds of nature.

Still, Mercedes cried a lot. She missed her husband and son. A judge realized it was too dangerous for her to return to El Salvador and granted her asylum. She got permission to stay and work in the United States. Then, she found a job at a hotel. Mercedes started saving every penny she could. Two years later, she sent for her family. Mercedes waited five agonizing weeks for them to arrive.

▲ **Immigrants visited the Los Angeles, California, U.S. Citizenship and Immigration Services building to get permission to live and work in the United States.**

For Mercedes, the reunion was a dream come true. But for her seven-year-old son, the United States was a nightmare. The war in El Salvador had frightened him and he was scared of many things. Loud noises made him tremble and hide in fear. It took years for him to finally feel safe.

Mercedes was nervous whenever she went back to El Salvador to visit her mother. The civil war had ended in 1992, but the violence continued with gang wars. The gang violence was the result of years of war. No one dared to complain about the gangs because they would be killed. Signs in the city warned people not to talk about what they saw. Young kids were asked to join the gangs, and if they refused, they were killed. Many families tried to flee the country. Mercedes' family in El Salvador didn't talk about the violence. They cherished their time together and tried to have fun.

When asked how she developed so much inner strength, Mercedes replied, "I had no choice. Life has so many things to give you, and you can either get stuck or move along. I feel like somehow I was able to move along."[1]

◄ **Although there's violence in El Salvador, people still take the time to celebrate festivals such as the Flower and Palm Festival.**

Chapter 2

JOURNEY TO THE UNITED STATES

At night, 13-year-old Armando would lie down, exhausted. At dawn, he dragged himself out of bed to go to work. He went to the fields to shovel dirt in the hot Guatemalan sun. Since his father had left for the United States, Armando was now the man of the house.

Even with the money he made, Armando's family often went hungry. The beans and tortillas his mother made for him and his younger sister barely kept them fed. Civil wars, a high population, and lack of education kept the Guatemalan people living in poor conditions for many years.

Armando remembered watching as his father prayed for something to change. Then, in 2010, his father left their little village in the mountains of Guatemala. His father had decided to work for eight years in the United States and save his money. Then he would return to Guatemala and give his family a better life. Armando dreamed of the day they would all be together again.

Armando took on another job delivering heavy loads of firewood. Sweat poured down his face as he worked in the afternoon sun, but this job was a big help to his family. The money also paid for the classes that Armando took on weekends. He was determined to finish his education.

As time went on, the amount of money his father was sending started to decrease. The pressure to work crushed Armando's dream of graduating from school. He made a decision to leave. One morning in 2014, he took a deep breath.

▲ **Guatemalan farmworkers work long hours in the hot sun.**

He hugged his mother and tried not to see the pain on her face. His little sister begged him not to go. He kissed her on the cheek and tasted the salt of her tears.

Armando was eager to begin his long trip. Without looking back, he closed the gate to his home and walked away from his family. He was ready to join his father. His journey began with a ride to the Guatemalan border. His fate was in the hands of a coyote the family had hired. Days later, Armando crossed into Mexico. Carrying fake Mexican **identification**, he arrived at a rundown house overflowing with immigrants.

Armando waited for days, sleeping on a mat and eating very little. Finally, it was his turn to cross the Rio Grande.

When he landed on the bank, a smuggler picked him up. He drove Armando across the U.S. border and dropped him off alongside the road. Thinking he was home free, Armando breathed a sigh of relief. But a few minutes later, U.S. immigration officials pulled up. Armando froze in fear.

▲ **At the Mexico-Guatemala border, immigrants try to cross the Suchiate River as part of their journey to the United States.**

The officials took him to a detention center in Texas. A detention center is a place where people are held for a period of time if they've illegally entered a country. Armando stayed there for a few days. Then he was moved to a shelter for immigrants. He lived there for 21 days.

One day, the officials let him go. They told Armando that he would have to go to court later. Armando's father needed him to work, so Armando went to Illinois. He got a job cleaning farm equipment at night. This left him with time to go to school during the day.

> "This is the place where there is no violence, as there is in my country."[2]
>
> —Emilia Figueroa, a Guatemalan woman who came to the United States

A few months later, Armando appeared at an **immigration court**, but he had no lawyer. The judge granted Armando more time to get a lawyer. A new court date was set. Armando wondered why it was so difficult to stay in the United States. He questioned whether he should leave the country and simply return to Guatemala.

◀ **Many Central American immigrants who reach the United States find themselves in Texas detention centers.**

Chapter 3

FIGHTING TO STAY

Maryori Urbina-Contreras cherished the photos of her mother. She would stare at the glossy photos and soak in the details of her mother's face. Maryori longed to hear her mother's voice over the phone, which was the only way they could communicate. When Maryori was eight months old, her mother had left Honduras to work in the United States to save money for her family.

◀ Police patrol some streets in Honduras, hoping to reduce the amount of violence in the country.

The young girl lived with her father in a crowded slum in Tegucigalpa, the country's capital city. Many people in Honduras were living in poor conditions. Maryori had to take a taxi to school because she wouldn't be safe on the bus. She played indoors with her cousins. She wasn't allowed to go outside alone.

Gang and drug violence exploded into Maryori's neighborhood in the mid-2000s. By 2011, her country had become one of the most dangerous in the world. Her father took her to a different neighborhood to live with her aunt, thinking she would be safer. But she wasn't. One day, Maryori was stunned with fear. As she was walking to school, a man pointed a gun at her and robbed her. A month later, she watched in horror as a man was shot in the middle of the street.

By the time she was 13, Maryori had seen enough violence and felt enough terror. Determined to find her mother in the United States, she decided to leave Honduras. One day in February 2014, Maryori packed her school bag with some clothes. She took the money she had saved from her allowance. She shut the front door behind her, telling no one that she was leaving for good. She didn't want anyone to know because she was afraid they would try to stop her.

▲ **Groups of Central American immigrants seek safety in the United States.**

Maryori had heard about a group of people who were planning to go to the United States. She met them at a café. By the time Maryori's aunt knew she was gone, Maryori was on a bus traveling north.

The group crossed into Guatemala and then into Mexico. Maryori slept on dirt floors when the groups rested for the night. She only had juice and crackers for meals. After four weeks, the group finally reached the U.S. border.

Maryori climbed on a raft and floated across the Rio Grande. She trudged up the steep bank. Then she gasped in fear as she looked straight into the eyes of a border patrol agent. The agent took Maryori into custody. He took her to a detention center in Texas and called her mother. Maryori's mother was frantic when she got the call. She desperately asked the immigration official, "Is my daughter alive?"[3] A month later, Maryori stepped off a plane in Chicago, Illinois. When she found her mother at the airport, Maryori raced over and wrapped her in a hug.

Maryori appreciated the quiet of her new home. She was not afraid to take the bus to school. She met her two half-sisters and they played in the park together. Maryori learned English quickly. After a few months, she was helping her English teacher with the other Spanish-speaking students.

Unaccompanied children taken into custody at the border were served with a notice to appear in immigration court. Maryori waited for her court date.

"This is a country of opportunities in a place where I am safe, where I feel like I am home. And I know that even though it's not the country where I was born, it's a place that can be my home."[4]

—*Maryori Urbina-Contreras*

21

CENTRAL AMERICAN IMMIGRANT POPULATION (1980-2015)

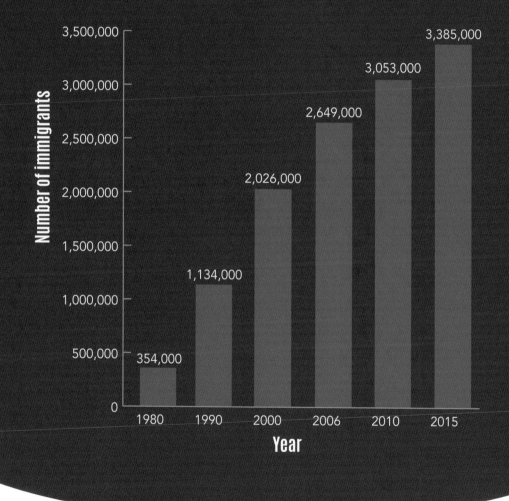

Luckily, a Chicago attorney had agreed to help her plead her case for asylum. Maryori had to explain to the judge that she might be killed if she returned to Honduras. Finally, the day of the hearing arrived in February 2018. Maryori stared silently out the window as she rode to the immigration court.

During a grueling two-hour interview, she answered every question honestly. She told the judge about the gang violence she had seen in Honduras and how she feared going back there. Then she waited anxiously for the decision. After only 15 minutes, the judge granted her asylum. With tears in her eyes, Maryori thanked her.

"I felt in danger. I knew I was exposed to danger and I knew that this person could kill me and was capable of doing that."[6]

— *Maryori Urbina-Contreras, speaking to the judge at her court date*

Outside the court, Maryori wrapped an American flag around her shoulders. Surrounded by her family, she said, "This is the flag that protects me. This is my home now."[5]

Chapter 4

SEPARATED FROM FAMILY

F ive-year-old José sat on a bed in an unfamiliar room. He folded his legs to his chest and tried to hold back tears. Before him lay two pieces of paper. He had drawn a picture of his family and a sketch of his dad because he missed them dearly. He kept the drawings under his pillow when he slept and wondered when he might hear from his family.

◀ Parents crossing the U.S.-Mexico border without permission were forced to give their children to U.S. government officials.

Weeks before, José and his father had fled the violence in Honduras. They had safely made it to Mexico and hoped for an even better life in the United States. In order to get into the United States, they illegally crossed the U.S.–Mexico border. U.S. government officials found them after they entered the country and took Jose's father into custody. The U.S. officials had to separate José from his father because children are not allowed in jail. Another official gave José to a woman, Janice, who took care of refugee children.

> "He holds onto the two pictures for dear life. . . . It's heart-wrenching."[8]
>
> —*Janice, speaking about José*

Janice knew the U.S. immigration laws made it difficult for families to stay together. She said, "I have nothing but sorrow and compassion for the families."[7] By providing meals and a safe home, Janice and others helped children like José while they were separated from their families.

Janice was kind to José. But she couldn't replace his parents. In the darkness of his new room at night, he stared at the wall.

▲ **People waited outside the United States, hoping to apply for asylum.**

José remembered living with his family in Honduras. Even at five years old, he knew it wasn't safe to be outside alone. There was violence right outside his family's door back home. People in the country also didn't have much money, which made it difficult to live there. José's time in Honduras affected his life in the United States. One day after José arrived at Janice's home, the sound of a firetruck scared him. His eyes widened, "La violencia, la violencia," he said.[9] Sirens and loud noises reminded José of the sound of gunshots in Honduras.

Many people from Central America were in the same situation as José and his family. They faced violence in their home country and sought a better life in the United States.

Unfortunately, entering the United States legally takes time and there's a process that needs to be followed.

If immigrants choose to avoid this process and enter the United States without permission, they risk being arrested. It is against the law to cross the border without permission. If parents are arrested for breaking the law, they can't bring their children to jail with them. In May 2018, more than 2,000 children were separated from their parents because of this. This is why José was separated from his father. Many Americans were upset that parents and children were separated, while others thought it was necessary to stop illegal immigration into the United States.

▲ **People went to the White House to protest children being separated from their parents.**

▲ **Children and parents were relieved when they were finally reunited.**

After spending days in his temporary home, José was still quiet. He spent time alone and didn't say much to Janice because he missed his family. One of the only things he said to her was, "When will I see my papá?"[10] But Janice couldn't tell him because, at the time, no one knew.

In mid-June, President Trump decided to stop separating families at the border. Instead, he chose to hold families together while they were being detained by U.S. officials. A judge ordered President Trump to reunite separated parents and children by the end of July 2018, and most were.

After families were reunited, some fought to stay in the United States. Others were forced to leave the country.

But before José knew he would see his father again, he struggled with his situation. In his room, José felt hot tears pour from his eyes. He reached under the pillow and felt around until he heard paper crinkling. Once his finger touched a bent corner of paper, he pulled out the two drawings of his family. They were wrinkled, so he smoothed the paper on his lap. He imagined his mom smiling at him and holding his father's warm hand. His parents had wanted him to find a better life in the United States, but José only wished his family was together.

THINK ABOUT IT

- Why do you think so many Central American immigrants choose to move to the United States instead of to other countries?
- Do you think countries should provide help to refugees? Explain your answer.
- What are some advantages and disadvantages of having people from different cultures live in the United States?

GLOSSARY

asylum (uh-SYE-luhm): Asylum is protection given to people who came from a dangerous area. Many Central Americans have come to the United States seeking asylum.

coyotes (koh-YOH-tez): Coyotes are people hired to smuggle immigrants into another country. Many Central Americans hire coyotes to get them safely across the border.

guerrilla (guh-RIL-uh): A guerrilla is a member of a small group that is fighting for a cause against larger forces. Guerrilla forces in Guatemala fought against the government.

identification (eye-den-ti-fuh-KAY-shun): Identification is a paper or card that tells who a person is. Some immigrants have carried fake identification.

immigration court (im-i-GRAY-shun KORT): An immigration court looks into the cases of people who have entered the United States and decides if they can stay in the country. Armando went to an immigration court.

persecution (pur-suh-KYOO-shun): Persecution is the act of punishing people based on their religion, race, gender, or other characteristics. Some people in Central America faced persecution.

rations (RASH-unz): Rations are fixed amounts of food because of a shortage. Some immigrants were fed small rations as they traveled.

refugees (ref-yoo-JEEZ): Refugees are people who seek safety in a foreign country, especially to avoid war or other dangers. Many refugees from Central America come to the United States.

SOURCE NOTES

1. "Immigrant Stories: Escaping Civil War in El Salvador." *Post Independent*. Swift Communications, 25 July 2016. Web. 17 July 2018.

2. John Burnett. "Inside the Trial of 3 Guatemalan Mothers Separated from Their Children." *NPR*. NPR, 8 June 2018. Web. 19 July 2018.

3. Colleen Mastony. "Honduran Teen, Who Entered U.S. as Unaccompanied Child, Awaits Word on Fate." *Chicago Tribune*. Chicago Tribune, 13 Nov. 2015. Web. 17 July 2018.

4. "Honduran Teen Makes Last Bid to Stay in U.S." *Chicago Tribune*. Chicago Tribune, n.d. Web. 17 July 2018.

5. Elvia Malagon. "Immigration Judge Grants Asylum to Honduran Teen-Activist Who Fled Gang Violence at 13." *Chicago Tribune*. Chicago Tribune, 1 Mar. 2018. Web. 17 July 2018.

6. Ibid.

7. Miriam Jordan. "'It's Horrendous': The Heartache of a Migrant Boy Taken from His Father." *New York Times*. New York Times Company, 7 June 2018. Web. 30 July 2018.

8. Ibid.

9. Ibid.

10. Ibid.

TO LEARN MORE

Books

Ada, Alma Flor. *Yes! We Are Latinos*. Watertown, MA: Charlesbridge, 2013.

Argueta, Jorge. *Somos Como Las Nubes = We Are Like the Clouds*. Toronto, ON: Groundwood Books, 2016.

Delacre, Lulu. *Us, in Progress: Short Stories about Young Latinos*. New York, NY: Harper, 2017.

Web Sites

Visit our Web site for links about Central American immigrants: childsworld.com/links

Note to Parents, Teachers, and Librarians: We routinely verify our Web links to make sure they are safe and active sites. So encourage your readers to check them out!

INDEX